Our Earthians Community Group

Stories of war, conflict and displacement

ARCHITECTURE

A Tapestry of 21 Voices

Things That Matter

An Ink Gladiators Press® Publication

First Published by Ink Gladiators Press®

ISBN 13: 978-93-49117-04-4

First Edition

Architecture

Book 1 of Things That Matter

Credits:

Compiled by Our Earthians Community Group
Silently Authored by Reena Doss
Edited and Proofed by Justin Adam Wolf and Aelius Arche
Book Design by Leonie Belle Hawk
Interior Art Direction and Development by Sinbad Ocean

Ink Gladiators Press®
Publishing and promoting warriors on life's battlefield
Founded in 2019 | Bangalore, India
www.inkgladiatorspress.com

For those who gather the facts, document the pain, and hold the mirror to the world—Human Rights Watch, for making sure the world cannot look away; Save the Children, for standing beside the smallest hands in the darkest hours; UNICEF, for amplifying the needs and rights of every child caught in the crossfire; UNESCO, for fighting to preserve culture, education, and memory when bombs try to erase them; UNHCR, for protecting the displaced and reminding us that every refugee is a person, not a number; Borderless World Foundation, for providing support to children in conflict zones, particularly in Jammu and Kashmir; and Global Protection Cluster, for tracking every checkpoint, every missing home, and every silenced voice. You are the Guardians of Truth. Thank you for illuminating what so many would rather leave in shadow. Your work becomes the foundation for stories that demand justice. Your reports become truth-telling tools. Your data becomes lifelines. You are the quiet teachers, the fierce mothers, the artists, the rebuilders and the rememberers. You make room for the type of grief that has no end. Your hands mend what war, destruction and displacement tried to steal.

For the children who remember too much, we see you—to the ones who slept beneath broken ceilings and dreamed in languages older than war; to the ones who carried keys in their pockets for doors the wind had already swallowed; to the ones who built kingdoms from cardboard, castles from tarp, and bridges from chalk; to the ones who named the stars after the gone, who planted stories in rubble; and who drew windows where there were none. We carry your names in prayers. We believe your dreams will bloom again. We listen and document because the world hasn't forgotten you.

For the Readers who pass on the stories by word of mouth, through stories, through posts, and in social circles.

May all that you lost find their way home.
May your own stories rise.
May your voices echo.

ARCHITECTURE is dedicated to all of YOU.

THINGS THAT MATTER

A Voice Tapestry

∞

There is no page numbering because Infinity marks our voices.

Architecture

Stories of War, Conflict & Displacement

Architecture is so much more than buildings standing tall or those that have crumbled to dust. Their structures hold stories—of lives lived, of homes loved, of futures dreamed, and futures stolen. **When war, conflict, and displacement rip through communities, it is architecture that carries the weight of loss and the echoes of resilience.** Every broken wall, every absent roof and every makeshift shelter becomes a story, each bearing witness to what was, what is, and what could be again.

Here, we have imagined hearing these stories through the voices of children—innocent witnesses to violence, destruction and upheaval. Their heartbreaking experiences are tender but the way they express themselves are fierce, fragile and unbreakable. Having had to grow up too fast, they seek refuge in architecture to express themselves through poetry, imagination and artistic creations. They see buildings not just as structures, but as living witnesses to their journeys: places that hold memory, strength, and the possibility of healing.

War shatter more than lives; they shatter homes. Bombed-out ruins and fractured landscapes become visible scars of violence, yet even absence speaks… A missing building, a flattened neighborhood, a vanished street tell us stories of erased histories and forced displacement.

A crumbled foundation is not just rubble, it has become the shattered security of a lost childhood and a stolen culture. For children, these broken places are monuments to grief and unforgettable testimony.

Architecture also tells stories about survival. Refugee camps and temporary shelters have become raw expressions of impermanence and endurance even though they can be overlooked or dismissed. Tents pitched on uncertain ground and makeshift homes crafted from scraps are not just shelters, but are voices crying out: "I deserve to belong."

In these fragile spaces, creativity, dreams and dignity persist. New ideas for humane, sustainable and healthier refugee housing offer glimmers of the future, challenging the world's indifference and promising a new beginning—one where displacement does not mean erasure or that refugees should be seen as a burden to their own as well as other nations.

Border walls loom large as architectural embodiments of division and control. They should be seen as the world's physical scars of occupation, fear, separation and exclusion. **A wall may seem impenetrable, but its cracks like the whispered stories of climbing, drawing, and dreaming beyond it—speak of rebellion.** In these transitional spaces, power is daily contested, directly and indirectly.

Memorial architecture stands as a different type of storyteller. These structures honor memory and truth. Monuments are built to remember victims of war, genocide, and ethnic cleansing and serve as collective witnesses that urge us to confront grief, history and responsibility. Whether heavy with silence or open to the sky, these structures tell stories that words themselves cannot fully express. They become places where societies face the ghosts of their past and search for paths to reconcile.

Beyond ruins and remembrance, there is also the powerful act of rebuilding. Reconstruction is not simply about blueprints, bricks, and mortar. It is, in fact, an act of defiance towards what occurred. When schools are reopened, homes are rebuilt, and cultural landmarks are restored, communities are declaring to the world: "We are still here."

Each rebuilt structure carries the pulse of freedom—a testament that even after devastation, identity and belonging can be reclaimed. For those who are forced to flee, home becomes something less tangible. But that doesn't mean it is less real.

∞

Migrants and displaced people often carry their homes in memories, stories, and symbols—places that exist between "where they were", "they're here" and "tomorrow's there". Through art, architecture, and portable spaces, they learn to weave new identities from the fragments of their past and the present. Mobile museums, storytelling shelters, and hybrid homes become living metaphors for movement, mental health and memory because they carry the underlying human need to belong, even when land, people and walls have failed them.

Through these forms and more, architecture speaks. It carries the voices of humanity and the children who remember too much but who imagine in bold colors. **It becomes a language of grief, trauma, denial, survival, exile, acceptance and…a homecoming.** In the silent spaces between bricks and broken windows, in the whispered stories of walls and tents, there is a quiet resistance—one that insists on living, on healing, and on joy.

Thus, Architecture becomes not only a witness, but a storyteller and hope dealer.

∞

A Cracked Wall

I will paint bright flowers for every crack…

Each crack appeared after a different explosion. Every day I sat beside the broken wall. It looked like a map—veins of whispered names, each one a silent echo of those who vanished like shadows. Some ran away when the bombs sang too close, some vanished beneath the weight of fear, but the wall remembers all the stories it holds for they are soft as breath.

One day, when the guns fall silent, **I will paint bright flowers for every crack**—red like courage, yellow like hope, blue like dreams that remain unbroken. I name the cracks after my friends as I hold their silence close, waiting for their laughter to come back.

Until that day, my fingers will trace the cracks.

Remnants: Ruins of a school
Description: Damaged. Fractured. Grief.

Renamed as **The Flower Room** by Dalia, Age 8

Fact: Over 25,000 schools have been damaged or destroyed by armed conflict in the last decade.

I will paint bright flowers for every crack...

Black Sky

The sky holds names I can't bury.

Sorrow is my roof. But at night, it disappears when I lie on my back and look up. Where the ceiling or clouds used to be, the velvet darkness feels welcoming. It's cold sometimes, but I like the stars. They can keep secrets.

The sky holds names I can't bury. I ask them if they know about the boy with the dimples, our neighbor with the kind laugh and the girl with the red dress. No one knows where their bodies are, but I know that their stars talk to them. I tell the stars to let them know what we ate, who cried today and who didn't.

They don't answer, but they never leave either and that's enough for me.

Remnants: A house torn open.
Description: Vast. Death. Holy.

Renamed as **Indigo Nights** by Enzi, Age 11

Fact: Thousands of war victims remain unidentified or unburied due to ongoing conflict.

Brick by Brick

Let this be a roof that never fails the homeless…

Every day I carry one brick from the ruins near our shelter. Just one. I clean it, stack it, whisper a wish—"Let this be a kitchen that feeds the hungry", "Let this be a roof that gives safety", or "Let this be a window that brings the morning."

No one told me to do it, but I do it every day. Every task is a prayer made with my heart, hands and spirit. Maybe someone will need these bricks. Maybe they'll feel the wishes inside them, like the warmth of a fire when they feel cold, scared and alone. Maybe I can't build fast enough, but I can do it steadily.

Every brick I lay out says, "I was here. I helped. I cared."

Remnants: Rubble and slabs of stone.
Description: Patient. Duty. Hopeful.

Renamed as **Wishing Bricks** by Chantal, Age 11

Fact: Post-war rebuilding can take decades, often with no government support.

roof
warmth
safe
warmth
safe

Broken Frame

...the sky likes learning how to see us where the glass once was.

There's a window with no glass, just a square of sky—blue-gray and sometimes, angry. I sit on the floor and stare through it like it's a TV showing me the real world.

Mama says we'll fix the broken window soon, but **I don't want it to be fixed.** The wind comes in and tells me stories. A bird once flew inside. I swear it looked at me and nodded like as though it understood. I think the sky likes learning how to see us where the glass once was. The stars visit at night. The moon fits perfectly in the corner. The sun blinds whenever it arrives behind the clouds.

Maybe this window is whole in a different way. Maybe this window doesn't like to look out. **Maybe this window lets the world come in.**

Remnants: A window frame with chips of glass left behind.
Description: Hollow. Bright. Open.

Renamed as **The World's Window** *by Rudra, Age 8*

Fact: War destroys over 100,000 homes annually in active conflict zones.

Cardboard House

Homes can bloom in exile too.

My house doesn't exist after it exploded, but I remember it. Every corner. Every crack. So I made a model from old boxes. Each room just the way it was. The smell of Amma's tea in the kitchen. The squeaky boards near my bed. I even drew the window that always let in the late afternoon sun.

I planted a seed in every room—mint, thyme, and wildflowers. Papa said they wouldn't grow, but one did. Just one. A tiny green leaf in the living room. It gave me a whole basket of hope. I talk to it every day. "Tell the other rooms that we're still here." Even if the world forgets, I will remember it for us.

Homes can bloom in exile too. They will grow tall and return to us.

Remnants: A house made of cardboard and seeds.
Description: Gentle. Thoughtful. Wildflower.

Renamed as **Replanted Home** *by Anas, Age 9*

Fact: Refugee children often recreate their homes through art and storytelling as a healing act.

Homes can
bloom
in exile too.

Ceiling of Stars

I hum a lullaby and tell the younger ones the stars taught it to me.

There's no roof, but that's okay. I think the stars are braver than the woods of the forest. They don't burn.

At night, I lie on my mat and tell the other kids beside me which stars will protect the people we love and miss the most. "That one's for you. That one's for Mama. That one's for the house we lost." Sometimes, I think I see the stars blink. Like they're watching. Like they care. **When the wind gets cold, I hum a lullaby and tell the younger ones the stars taught it to me.** They believe me because they smile and fall asleep happy. I don't let them see my tears. But I know the stars do. They twinkle extra bright, just for me.

We don't need a roof. We have the whole sky holding us close.

Remnants: Only the sky and ground remain.
Description: Bare. Bright. Protective.

Renamed as **Star Watcher** by *Tariq, Age 7*

Fact: In war-torn regions, many families sleep in open air due to housing destruction.

Checkpoint Dreams

I wish Papa will walk through," I whisper to each door.

There are walls that swallow the road. Every morning we wait beside them at different places. The sun crawls up our backs like we are growing older too fast. I don't like the men with the guns. Why do they look through us like we are ghosts? Is it because we are painted with gray dust? Maybe that's why I carry colors in my pocket.

When no one is looking, I draw doors on the walls—blue like the sea my father told me stories about, with handles and a welcome mat made of stars and suns. "I wish Papa will walk through," I whisper to each door. My brother says the walls can't hear us, but I think they listen. I talk to them when I'm alone. I tell them my father's name so they will let him pass through. I tell them the stories he used to tell me, especially the ones that end with everyone getting a happily ever after.

One day, the walls will forget to stop us. One day, God will remember my wishes. **One day, the doors will open.**

Remnants: Concrete walls scribbled with words and art.
Description: Blocked. Haunted. Watched.

Renamed as **The Painted Passage** *by Wasim, Age 10*

Fact: Over 70 countries use physical checkpoints to restrict civilian movement in conflict zones.

Colored Chalk

They can wipe out the lines, but not the way I move.

The checkpoint has big gray blocks like sleeping giants. They're ugly and mean-looking, but they can't stop my chalk**. I draw hopscotch grids on every one. Red, blue, yellow.** Each square is a magic step—an entry to my old classroom, to the sea, to a world where no one points guns.

Sometimes, a soldier watches me. I don't stop. I just keep jumping. My feet make tapping music against the stone. I pretend that if I reach the last square, the wall will someday fall. **Perhaps my steps will turn into a path so bright even grown-ups will want to follow it.** They can wipe out the lines, but not the way I move. Not the way I hope.

My feet will draw a map no war machine can erase.

Remnants: Blocks, marked with color.
Description: Helpless. Games. Playful.

Renamed as **A Lit Map** *by Eshe, Age 9*

Fact: Conflict restricts millions of children from reaching school safely each day.

End Of Nowhere

We stood at the edge once, toes close to nothing.

The bridge used to go all the way across. Now it just stops. **Did someone erase the second half with a giant hand?**

We stood at the edge once, toes close to nothing. The wind pushed at our backs like it wanted us to leap. Instead, **we went home and made our own bridge.** Out of cardboard. Out of tape. Out of all the stories we could remember. We built it in the air with our mouths, each sentence another plank. Anand told the one about the bird that led his uncle to safety. I told the one about the ferry made of stars. And when it was finished, we crossed it laughing together, not falling.

Stone breaks. But stories? They hold.

Remnants: Half a bridge, reaching into sky.
Description: Cut. Dangling. Reimagined.

Renamed as **The Story Bridge** *by Asha, Age 10*

Fact: Infrastructure is a frequent target in war, cutting off access to aid, family, and safety.

Pocket Of Stones

They were just stones, but in my hands, they felt like memory.

On the day I had to flee with my Aunt, I had five stones in my coat pocket. I'd collected them earlier while playing, slipping them in without thinking and forgot that they were there. Later, on the road, my fingers found them again. They'd grown warm and smooth like as though they'd been waiting for me. I pulled them out, one by one, and gave each of them a name. I named them after the elements and imagined they were protectors of the places I loved, those places I had to leave behind.

One was for my home, where the curtains danced in the breeze and Mama sang while sweeping. **One was for my best friend,** who walked with me to the bus stop every morning, our feet always finding the same cracks in the sidewalk. **One was for the bakery,** where the old man handed me a warm bun just because he said he'd watched me grow. **One was for the hospital,** where Mama was waiting, her belly round with the twins that never got to be born. **And one was for my school,** where I always left a bit of my lunch for the three dogs who waited by the wall. They were just stones, but in my hands, they felt like memory. **Like a home I could carry.** Every night, I take them out and line them up on the windowsill. Sometimes, I pretend they are the places. "This one is the schoolyard. This one is the tree with long vines. This one smelled like bread. This one sings like Mama. This one is Papa's coat." I don't cry anymore. I just remember.

I think one day I'll plant them in the ground. Maybe the stones will remember how to become a village. One that only I know how to find.

Remnants: Five stones of memory.
Description: Small. Elemental. Portable.

Renamed as **The Pocket Village** *by Rami, Age 10*

Fact: Children often retain the most vivid and precise mental maps of places that no longer exist.

∞

Suitcase Roofs

I can see inside—my home, not the one I lost, but the one I haven't met yet.

I wanted to build a city in the middle of the camp. I knew I could not build it from bricks, but there were so many suitcases and travel bags to use instead. Big ones, small ones, some with stickers from places I don't think I'll ever get to see. Some had clothes, spoons and photo frames. I stacked them carefully. I hope they forgot who they used to be because I made each of them into a home. This colorful one is a kitchen. That green one is a window. In this tall one, a family lives there with two laughing kids and a kitten that was never given away.

A woman who shares her bread with me tells me repeatedly not to play with them, but I tell her just as insistently, "These aren't just travel bags. They're homes!" That's when she smiles. Sometimes, I think she says it because she wants to hear my answer even when she does not believe in my words. But I do.

My home is the tallest. It has a roof made of big dreams. Sometimes, when the sun hits just right, I can see inside—my home, not the one I lost, but the one I haven't met yet. A man walking past laughed under his breath. "Keep building," he says. "Maybe they will turn into castles."

"Yes," I tell him, "One day, I will live inside them."

Remnants: A cluster of castle dreams and imagined lives.
Description: Carried. Places. Future.

Renamed as **Gypsy Houses** *by Kunal, Age 8*

Fact: There are over 36 million child refugees globally.

BIG DREAMS
MY HOME

Tarp Home

My imagination keeps us strong, because I fill it with dreams.

It started with one tarp and four sticks. My sister held one side while I tied the knots with our shoelaces. **Now we have a palace.** It wobbles when the wind blows, and when it rains, the floor becomes a sea. But inside, it is warm. It has secret rooms, a board we turned into a drawbridge, and a guard tower made from a broken chair. My sister is the Queen and I am her knight.

People say it's just a tarp, but they don't see the moat. They don't hear the trumpet sound when we raise our flag we made out of a t-shirt. **At night, we tell stories by flashlight.** Monsters can't get in, not even the real ones.

My imagination keeps us strong because I fill it with dreams.

Remnants: Blue plastic, odds and ends.
Description: Makeshift. Leaky. Temporary.

Renamed as **The Magical Palace** by Jamila, Age 7

Fact: Most refugee camps are made from materials meant to last weeks—but some remain for decades.

Temporary Roof

The canvas talks, if you know how to hear it…

I may live under cloth, with four poles and rope as its only anchors, but every pole has a name. That one is Capella. That one's Orion. This one is Vega and my favorite one here is Mira. I named them after stars because they're the only things that stay.

My tent flaps and coughs when the wind howls, but I sit inside and listen. **The canvas talks, if you know how to hear it**—Papa's voice calls me in for dinner, my older brother teases Mama's new hairstyle and the sound of the door we lost creaks open. Sometimes, I press my ear to the fabric. I imagine the tent rising higher, until it becomes a part of the sky, the place where no storm can rip apart and no family can be taken from me.

It is comforting to know my roof is made of stars.

Remnants: Canvas stretched beneath the stars.
Description: Flimsy. Familiar. Sacred.

Renamed as **The Star Tent** *by Trisha, Age 10*

Fact: Some refugee families spend over 10 years in temporary shelter.

MIRA

The Box House

I walk in circles, touching the same walls over and over again.

Our house has no doors. Not anymore. Papa said it's safer this way—no one in, no one out. The windows are shut tight too. The air is heavy like it forgot how to move.

I walk in circles, touching the same walls over and over again. But at night, when no one's watching, I take a piece of chalk and draw doors. **Doors only open in dreams, but that's okay.** One is by the kitchen. One near the bed. And a little one just for the cat we had to leave behind. Sometimes I knock on them softly and pretend someone knocks back.

In dreams, we left without being afraid.

Remnants: Four walls, sealed by fear.
Description: Still. Silent. Safe.

Renamed as **Invisible Doors** *by Duria, Age 8*

Fact: Many families in occupied zones seal homes for safety, creating invisible prisons.

The Hidden Stairs

If I climb down far enough, I'll find a place where time never broke.

I found them under the rubble—spiral stairs made of stone, leading down like a secret. I haven't told anyone. They'd say it's just ruins but I know better. **I know they lead somewhere. Somewhere quiet. Somewhere peaceful.** Somewhere where the sky never cracked and the clocks still tick…soft and slow.

Sometimes I sit on the top step and close my eyes. I imagine going down and down until I reach a door. **Behind it is a world before the bombs. Before goodbyes. Before heartbreaks.** If I climb down far enough, I'll find a place where time never broke. When the noise gets too loud, the stairs are always there—waiting like an open book no one else sees.

I'm not ready to go yet, but I have to be.

Remnants: A staircase under rubble.
Description: Secret. Twisting. Escape.

Renamed as **The Mysterious Stairs** *by Sara, Age 9*

Fact: Children in war zones often experience time distortion, trauma, and dissociation.

I FOUND
A PLACE
WHERE
TIME
NEVER
BROKE

The House That Disappeared

If I draw it enough times, maybe the land will remember.

Every morning, I find the same patch of ground—the one that doesn't have bricks anymore. **Just sky, air and dust.**

I kneel and drag my finger through the mud. First, the square for the front room, then the kitchen where Mama made soup, then the tiny room where my sister used to sing to a teddy bear she had to leave behind. I draw the door last, the one that always creaked like Grandfather's knees. Sometimes the wind comes and erases it, like it never mattered. **But I draw it again. And again. If I get it right… If I remember every corner…** If I draw it enough times, maybe the patch of ground will remember… Maybe Mama will laugh again. Maybe we'll hear the roosters. Maybe I'll see Papa's shoes by the door.

I press my hand into the dirt, where the stairs used to be. My palm leaves a print, like the house is holding my hand back. **It whispers, "I remember." I say, "Me too." Because someone has to.**

Remnants: A dirt patch where a house once stood.
Description: Vanished. Remembered. Yearning.

Renamed as **The House in My Hands** by Saad, Age 9

Fact: 1 in every 3 people displaced by war are children who have lost their homes.

If I draw it enough times . . .

The Key Necklace

I will plant this dream one day, like a seed.

I've never seen Grandmother's house, but I wear her key like a necklace. It warms my skin when I think about her. **She said that it opened a sunset colored door with bright flowers painted on it.** Behind that door were lemon trees and a fig that dropped sweet fruit right into your hands. She said the walls smelled of jasmine soap. I believe her.

Sometimes, I draw it—the house, because I want to remember Grandmother. I add a garden in the backyard and a swing tied to an olive branch. But in my version, doors don't need keys. **I want to leave all the doors unlocked.** I will plant this dream key one day, like a seed. And homes will bloom from the ground.

"My key will fit," I tell myself. "It's just waiting for the right soil."

Remnants: A rusted key to a door.
Description: Heavy. Remembered. Seeds.

Renamed as **The Dream Garden** *by Lina, Age 11*

Fact: Many displaced survivors of war still carry physical keys to homes they may never see again.

The Library With No Books

I write the stories I remember and the ones I invent…

It used to smell like dust and ink but it was my favorite place. The librarian knew my name. The shelves whispered poems if you listened. Now, it's just black. Charred walls. Empty air.

But I still write. On cardboard. On leaves. On the back of old posters. My older sister said we may have lost everything, but I didn't lose my words. I like making spelling mistakes on purpose. **Words are broken into pieces, bitten from other words and borrowed from other languages anyway,** yet they are seen as whole and belong to those who create, use and teach them to us.

I write the stories I remember and the ones I invent—about dragons who rebuild schools and mermaids who speak languages made of rain. I hide them in nooks and crevices. Some I bury like seeds.

They live in me now, growing roots in the silence.

Remnants: Ashes where shelves used to be.
Description: Burned. Quiet. Rewritten.

Renamed as **The Rooted Library** *by Amara, Age 12*

Fact: Libraries and schools are often looted or destroyed in wartime to suppress education.

I write stories
I rønnember
and the ones
invent

The Standing Door

...some things are just waiting to be remembered.

It's a door in the middle of a field. No walls. No house. Just standing there, like it forgot what it was for. But I found it, and now I visit every day. I open it. I close it. I knock on it. **I whisper the names of the dead into the crack where the doorknob used to be—"Karol," "Quentin."**

Sometimes I imagine it leads to a hallway full of cake or to a playroom full of my sister's dolls. People say it's just made of wood. But I think **some things are just waiting to be remembered.**

Maybe this door was waiting too.

Remnants: An upright door with no hinges.
Description: Still. Expectant. Worn.

Renamed as **The Forgotten Door** *by Ansh, Age 4*

Fact: Abandoned structures often become symbolic altars for returning families.

Karol
Quentin

The Watchtower's Shadow

I asked Mama if towers get lonely. She said it's possible.

There's a tower on the hill with metal bones and dark glasses. It never sleeps. It watches our rooftops, our games and even the way we whisper. I don't like walking near it. **It feels like the sky has a spy.** Even the birds don't sing there.

In my dreams, I plant vines that grow fast so I climb up to the top and hang Terra's bells from its neck. Terra used to like the sound they made when she grazed in the fields. **Should I ring Terra's bells loud enough to make the tower feel again?** Perhaps towers get tired of standing guard. Perhaps towers are too far away to be heard. Perhaps towers never know which music to dance to.

I asked Mama if towers get lonely. She said it's possible. **I left a paper flower at its base, just in case.**

Remnants: Only the sides remain—like eyelids without eyes.
Description: Cold. Tall. Unblinking.

Renamed as **The Sleeping Tower** *by Nitya, Age 11*

Fact: Surveillance architecture is used in over 50 conflict zones to control populations.

Whispering Ruins

If we listen closely, the past will teach us to rebuild.

The old archways still stand. Kind of. They lean like my tired grandparents, but they don't yet fall. I walk past them every day, and **if the wind is quiet enough, I hear things**—spices being measured, a woman laughing and a man calling out for pomegranates.

Papa says the market is gone, but I think it left whispers behind. Ghostly ones. Songs and smells live in my memory. Sometimes I close my eyes and walk slowly because I want to feel the stories touch me. Maybe if I can find and gather the lost threads, I can sew them into a tapestry so it all feels like home again. There are so many buried secrets I have to learn how to listen to.

I think the archways know where I must begin.

Remnants: The bones of a marketplace
Description: Broken. Echoing. Remembered.

Renamed as **The Haunted Bazaar** *by Sama, Age 10*

Fact: Cultural sites are deliberately destroyed in war to erase identity.

Not All Warriors Shout

Peace Is Not Passive

When the peace within you becomes louder than the outward peace around you, you begin to realize just how much stronger you've become from within. The world may say and do a million things differently—pressuring, demanding, expecting you to conform to its noise, its experiences, its rhythm—but if you can still rise amidst all that chaos, **if you can take a stand for your voice,** for the freedom to choose when, where and why you speak through whatever gifts you were given, for the right to express yourself (based on your mental health or current place in life) and for the fire that burns in you to be used for others' good—**then you are demonstrating a vision of peace few will ever understand.**

This is a peace forged not from comfort, but in trial. This is a peace you choose even when the opposite might feel easier or more justified. This is a peace that searches for every possible road to healing before ever reaching for conflict. It's not born from silence or avoidance, but is the result of surviving personal wars where violence—whether emotional, verbal, or physical—could have been the easier choice. It is gained after lying buried for months or years in the dirt, by crawling through dark tunnels, by scraping the blackest coal from your body in a mine no one else has ever walked through and still choosing the liberation of peace as your way forward. The hearts of those who impulsively throw stones first are often lost in their own pain.

Righteous anger over injustice is good—but anger in the name of justice, when not rooted in long-term solutions and peace, often rises from deeper, unresolved triggers. Those who don't confront that before gearing up for justice will project their pain onto others with different views, beliefs, or perspectives, using the cause of justice as a shield to mask inner turmoil. But **those who walk the path of peace, those who wield it as their most persistent, patient, and powerful shield, will often provoke discomfort**—especially in those who thrive on planting dissent and division, not seeds of healing and hope.

Peace, when chosen consciously and with strength, is not a weakness. In fact, it is a bold defiance against the cycles of harm and history—and it is a weapon more enduring than any rage could ever be. Peace is the shield that chooses to be stronger than the noise.

Not all warriors shout, some speak in words, art, creativity, and in prayers.

∞

Between Borders and Bombs

The Youngest Witnesses: A Global Snapshot of Conflict

In 2025, war continues to shape the world—not just through headlines or maps, but through the eyes and hearts of children. Their stories are not always told, but they are everywhere: whispered in refugee camps, etched in broken school walls, or carried quietly in the corners of dusty suitcases.

In Gaza, children live in a world of rubble and hunger. After more than 600 days of war, the smell of bread is rare, and silence never lasts long. Most have lost family members, their homes, or both. Some haven't eaten in days. Aid barely gets through. The sky above them is loud, and there are few places to hide.

In Sudan, children have been torn from their homes by a brutal civil war. In Darfur, many sleep under trees or in shelters made of plastic sheeting. Some no longer speak much—they've seen too much. Others draw pictures in the sand of the homes they miss.

In the Democratic Republic of the Congo, children run from bullets and recruitment. They carry water instead of books, and many no longer remember what peace feels like. Rebels take what they want, and often, that includes the young.

And closer to home, the conflict between India and Pakistan reignited this May. As someone from India, I cannot speak on this without feeling outrage—but I will try to be as objective as possible. After India launched missile strikes on Pakistan following a deadly attack in Kashmir, children on both sides felt the tremors. Some lost parents. Some hid in fear as sirens rang out. Later, after a school bus was bombed in Balochistan and dozens of children were injured, the Balochistan Liberation Army (BLA) as well as several government officials from Pakistan decided to blame the Indian army.

Frankly, I find that outrageous and insulting. When the Indian army has continued to respect the lives of children, women, and innocent civilians on both sides even in times of conflict for decades, it is hard for me to understand how anyone could point the finger at them when it is known that the province of Balochistan has been home to "a decades-long bloody insurgency" by BLA. In my view, the Indian army have shown remarkable restraint and professionalism despite the complexity, challenges of the situation and repeated provocations.

Then there are many people from Pakistan who live in India, contribute proudly, and call it home. It's painful to see how some here view their presence as unwelcome as if they don't belong. Some voices insist citizenship should be defined by religion, which only fuels division. Unfortunately, religious fanaticism has been rising in many places, but not everyone supports violence or division. This conflict is not about religion, it's about the struggle for land and power.

Terrorism, in all forms, is abhorrent. Mocking entire nations because of ongoing wars is abhorrent because it fuels mass rage in people who do not have access to the facts. Generalizing hatred toward innocent civilians just because they come from another country is abhorrent. Armies reflect the kind of leadership that governs a country. That is because they are obligated to follow orders that their leaders take and they have to trust that they are not being led to commit crimes against humanity. Armies who engage in war only when it becomes an absolute necessity have my full respect. That is because they are choosing to **honor life, peace and community** more than being responsible for loss, chaos and violence. Armies sacrifice their lives daily to keep us safe from external threats. That is why those who wield power over them must first practice restraint, have self-discipline and really think about the long-lasting effects of war for the nation that they serve and how their citizen will be received in the world after the decisions they make. **I salute, stand with, and honor all nations, Earthians, and catalysts** who choose the path of peace, who defend the rights of the innocent, and who reject the manipulations of evil that terrorism uses to distort healthy patriotism, sever bonds of shared humanity, and enforce thoughtless labels.

UNICEF has constantly been calling on leaders to remember the promises made in the United Nations Convention on the Rights of the Child (UNCRC)—to protect, to shelter, to keep safe. No one knows when the next war might come, or which unseen forces are fueling the tensions and deepening the cycle of hate. But children know this: when grownups go to war, it is the young who bleed first. Many no longer sleep through the night. Their drawings show tanks, death and helicopters instead of trees, houses and stars. **But the question remains: who listens when a child calls for peace?**

Across continents and conflict zones, one truth echoes: children are not just bystanders in war—they are **survivors**, **dreamers**, and in many cases, **the most powerful witnesses** to what the world chooses to forget.

Sources: AP News, The Guardian, Wikipedia, UNICEF, United Nations & Save the Children

∞

Things That Matter

Living Voices of Truth

Our voices are more than just sound. They are how we leave a mark on the world.

Whether we speak through words, paint with color, illustrate through art, capture feelings through photos, craft with our hands, tell stories on stage, move through dance, or sing out a melody—our voice is our truth.

It's how we say, "I'm here. I feel. I matter." And that matters deeply.

When we create through poetry, art, writing, music, stories, photography, or performance, we are giving life to what we carry inside.

Our hopes. Our fears. Our dreams.

Creativity is how we make sense of the world and how we connect with others who feel the same. It's how we show love, protest injustice, celebrate joy, and imagine something better. Our children need to grow up in a world where their voices are not just heard, but encouraged. A world that says:

"You can tell your story. You can create something beautiful. Your voice counts."

When they write, create, express, compose, art, exaggerate, or sing, they are not just playing—they are building their identity, their courage, and their future. And our planet, with all its wild beauty—its forests, oceans, and skies—need our voice too. Through writing, art and storytelling, we remind each other of what we're losing and what's still worth fighting for.

Nature speaks in quiet ways. Our job is to help carry its message loudly, boldly and clearly.

There's so much going on in the world—war, inequality, climate change, mental health struggles. It can feel overwhelming, like one voice can't be enough.

But that's not true. When one person speaks, it gives another person courage.

When we share what matters to us, it creates a ripple. And enough ripples can create real waves of change.

That's why *Our Earthians Community Group* created the **Things That Matter** chapbooks—small collections of stories, lyrics, feelings, poems, art, photos, and thoughts from people of all ages and backgrounds. These little books are big in meaning. They are living voices that are meant to inspire your heart in the deepest of ways. They carry small voices with big truths. They are pages of power. They say:

"You're not alone. You deserves a place." They validate every voice, no matter how quiet, young, or different.

So whether your voice comes through a lens, a line of poetry, a canvas, a dance, or a song—**let it out.** Let it be loud or gentle, joyful or aching, raw or refined. What matters most is that it is yours.

And when we bring our voices together, that's when the world truly starts to listen.

Acknowledgements

We are grateful

From the Heart of the Author

Thank you to my *Beloved Weaver (or Heavenly Father)* of the Celestial Sky.

I cherish, adore, and honor you above all Earthly homes, temporary things, and my fading life itself. Thank you for my eyes, hands, and gifts of creativity. Help me to keep using them for others.

Thank you for everything; without you, I would be a ship that didn't know how to sail.

With love, joy, and gratitude,

Reena Doss

From Our Earthians Community Group

We thank *Reena Doss* for researching facts, compiling a tapestry of voice perspectives, and authoring these pieces accordingly.

We appreciate *Justin Adam Wolf* for his top-notch editing skills, and *Aeilus Arche* for his keen proofreading eyes. Our gratitude goes to *Leonie Belle Hawk* for her dedication to book design, layout, and formatting of this book, in close collaboration with *Sinbad Ocean*, who led the art direction and development of the interior visual structure.

And lastly, thank you to all those who do what they do and continue to inspire us to keep making a difference.

We remain at your service,

Our Earthians Community Group

Our Earthians Community Group

We belong to the earth, not just one part

Does your heart consistently call you a writer, poet, author, lyricist, photographer, artist, or creative? Then listen to its rhythm. Our Earthians Community Group was founded to acknowledge the storms of adversity—to give the wild that grows from them a place to exist, to grow, and to become. It is a space that brings together the voices of a community speaking as one.

We are deeply grateful for the journey that has shaped us—for the lessons, trials, and resilience that have guided us toward a greater vision through the work of our hands.

Through the publications of Ink Gladiators Press®, it is our hope that humanity reshapes the way we see one another—by finding courage in the most vulnerable, by giving voice to our hardest experiences, and by choosing to be seen, heard, and felt in the ways that come most naturally to us. This is because we are more than enough at every stage of growth.

Every piece we select, every book we review, and every creative we appreciate is not solely based on quality, uniqueness, or form—but on the belief that your voice matters.

Our mission is to connect writers, poets, artists, lyricists, photographers, visionaries, and communities across the world.

Through our global creative network, we continue to publish voices of expression, create meaningful collaborations, and hold space for mental health awareness through our various initiatives.

A Chapbook Series by Our Earthians Community Group

Things That Matter

Make your voice heard—whether it's your own, for someone else, or a cause you stand for.

Through the **Things That Matter** chapbook series, we invite you to empower conversations with hope, share stories with faith, inspire connections with dreams, and revolutionize change with love. Together, we can turn the impossible into possible journeys—one heartfelt step at a time. And most importantly, never give up.

Let's create ripple effects where kindness, understanding, and social impact take root, breathe and flourish like seeds that become beautiful gardens for the present and future generations to blossom in.

#ThingsThatMatter #InkGladiatorsPress #BeHeard

Follow us online to stay updated on publishing opportunities at Ink Gladiators Press®.

INK GLADIATORS PRESS

Publishing and promoting warriors on life's battlefield

We serve the creative community as a whole. We are passionate about publishing, promoting, and preserving the voices of authors, writers, artists, poets, lyricists, photographers, philosophers, editors, designers, storytellers, mental health advocates, and creators.

Our vision is to create a space where authors, professionals, and creatives can grow together by contributing their heart songs to humanity—gifts of inspiration through which new realities can be shaped through the art of dream-making.

We welcome your voices and expressions, and invite you to find a home with the Ink Gladiators family through our anthologies, workshops, and other supportive avenues.
When we come together with faith, hope, and love, everything is possible. We appreciate your love for reading and for being a part of our journey.

Thank you for being here.

Ink Gladiators Press®
www.inkgladiatorspress.com
Email: contact@inkgladiatorspress.com.

Please scan the QR Code below if you would like to follow us on Instagram @inkgladiatorspress.

www.ingramcontent.com/pod-product-compliance
Lightning Source LLC
Chambersburg PA
CBHW062113160726
48282CB00026B/784
9789349117044